Hindu
faith and practice

SECOND EDITION

Brian ... loff

The Hindu faith

One must believe in certain things with mind, heart and soul; and then live by them in the course of everyday life. Faith is always personal and individual. Each person follows the faith they choose. Here are some main parts of the Hindu faith.

Hindu beliefs

▶ There is One God, with many different parts, or forms.

▶ There are many ways to worship God and that each person is free to find his own way to worship.

▶ The universe undergoes endless cycles of creation, preservation and destruction.

▶ Each individual creates his own destiny by thoughts, words and deeds. This is called karma.

▶ There is no eternal hell and no damnation.

▶ Each soul is born over and over again (reincarnation) until it can perfect itself and become one with God (moksha).

▶ All souls will eventually become one with God and be freed from going through the cycle of rebirth.

▶ Mandir worship, rituals, festivals and personal devotion can all create a communion with God.

▶ Personal discipline, good conduct, purification, self-inquiry and meditation can all help us to know God and become closer to the goal of moksha.

▶ All life is sacred.

▶ All genuine religious paths are equal and deserve tolerance and understanding.

▶ Hindu scripture and teachings tell how to live a good and moral life, and how to become closer to God.

Find out more

Look at the companion Curriculum Visions book, 'Hindu mandir'.

Curriculum Visions

Hindu mandir

Lisa Magloff

Contents

What it means to be a Hindu 4

Brahma, Vishnu and Shiva 8

Mahadevi and the goddesses 10

Avatars of Vishnu and Ganesha... 12

Murtis and shrines 14

Puja 16

Aarti.. 18

Sacred texts.................................... 20

A Hindu way of life 24

Personal symbols 26

Hindu celebrations........................ 28

Glossary.. 30

Index.. 32

As you go through the book, look for words in **BOLD CAPITALS**. These words are defined in the glossary.

 Understanding others

Remember that other people's beliefs are important to them. You must always be considerate and understanding when studying about faith.

Individual worship.

What it means to be a Hindu

A Hindu believes that there are many paths to reaching the goal of being at one with God.

HINDUISM is one of the oldest faiths in the world and is practised by over one billion people, the majority of whom are in India. Within Hinduism is a huge variety of beliefs and practices. You can see this in a saying from an ancient **HINDU** religious scripture, the **RIG VEDA**: "Truth is One, though the paths to it are many." From this you can see that Hindus believe there are many paths which lead to God.

Basic beliefs

There are hundreds of **GODS AND GODDESSES** in Hinduism, but Hindus believe that these are all different forms of one Supreme God, called **BRAHMAN**. Because it is impossible to know the Supreme God, most people instead worship the different forms of God, which are called gods and goddesses.

There is no founder of Hinduism, no Heaven or Hell, no standard creed and no standard rituals. Instead, what lays at the root of Hinduism is the belief in **REINCARNATION**, or rebirth. This teaches that each **SOUL** is reborn over and over again in an endless cycle. Only by breaking free of this cycle can we join with God to achieve eternal peace and bliss.

Hinduism teaches that all souls eventually join with God. Each soul is free to find his own way to do this. Devotion and worship, living simply, practising **MEDITATION** and **YOGA**, and serving others can all help lead us closer to God.

Most Hindus worship at home. But for many, the **MANDIR**, or temple, is also important. Hindus respect and listen to holy men, called **GURUS**, or teachers, who have dedicated their lives to worship and devotion.

Gods and the cosmic force

Although Hindus believe that there is a Supreme God, they also believe that God can be worshipped in an almost endless number of ways.

So, each person, family and community worships the gods and goddesses they are most comfortable with. Because every god and goddess is a part of God, worshipping them is a way of forming a more personal and direct relationship with the Supreme God.

▼ These people are worshipping in a mandir. They are listening to a PRIEST say prayers and make offerings to the main god and goddess worshipped in this mandir.

Weblink: www.CurriculumVisions.com

The gods and goddesses are a visible reminder of God. Each person worships the gods and goddesses that he or she believes directly influence his or her life.

All religious paths lead to the same goal, the worship of God. We can see this in the following Hindu prayer: "Like all the rain waters that fall flow through the rivers to the same ocean, let all my prayers to various forms of the Divine ultimately flow to the same Almighty Lord."

Hindu values

There are four principles which guide one through life:

1. Following the traditions of Hinduism (**DHARMA**).
2. Achieving success (**ARTHA**).
3. Making the correct actions and decisions (**KARMA**).
4. Finding salvation or **ENLIGHTENMENT** (**MOKSHA**).

Each of these must be kept in mind as each person makes their way through life. Understanding how best to accomplish each of these is the first step to achieving salvation.

Hindu dharma

The word dharma is a **SANSKRIT** word that means 'a path which leads to God'. So, dharma can be thought of as the path to God. Dharma includes the teachings in Hinduism's sacred books, along with the traditions and practices of Hindus. Some of the traditions that are a part of Hindu dharma are a belief in karma, belief in God, belief in **NON-VIOLENCE**, belief in self-discipline, worship practices such as **PUJA** and having compassion for others.

Karma

The word karma means actions. Because each soul is born over and over again, the things we do in this life can affect what happens to us in the next life. Just like the things we did in our last life affect our life now. This is called the **LAW OF KARMA**.

▼ Bowing is one way to show devotion to the gods and goddesses.

For example, if we help someone in this life, then something good will happen to us, either now or in a future life. If we do something bad now, then something bad will happen to us later on. This is the same idea as the Christian saying, "You reap what you sow." This means we have to be very careful in what we do because we are responsible for everything that happens to us.

Hindu dharma teaches that we will be reincarnated time after time until all bad karma (bad deeds and bad thoughts) are replaced by good karma. When that happens, we will be ready to join God.

Artha

Artha means wealth, and Hinduism recognises that money is important in life. But this does not mean that we should only care about money and stop caring about others. Instead, artha means that everyone has a duty to take care of their family and others – and wealth is necessary for this.

For example, every family needs money in order to make sure that everyone in the family has good education and good health. Hindu dharma teaches that living simply is important, but also that we all have a responsibility to take care of our everyday needs.

Artha also means other kinds of wealth, for example, friendship, knowledge and love are also kinds of wealth.

Moksha

The goal of Hinduism is to stop being reincarnated and to reach God. This is also called achieving salvation or enlightenment, or **MOKSHA**.

Dharma, artha and karma guide our lives and help us to achieve moksha. Worshipping the gods and goddesses is another way to achieve moksha.

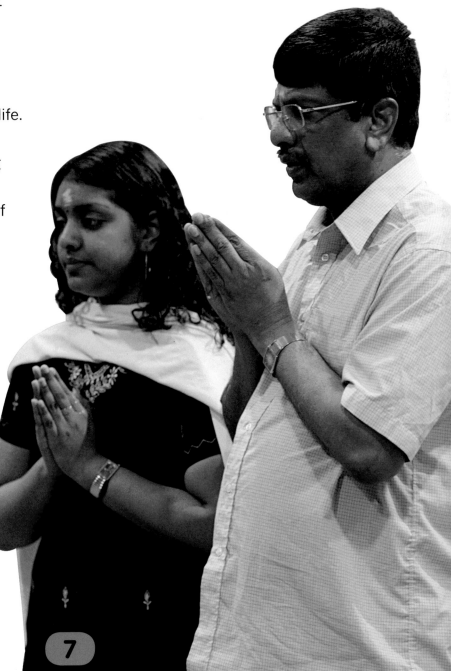

▶ Worship is an important part of Hindu dharma.

Brahma, Vishnu and Shiva

These three gods are called the TRIMURTI, the trio of great gods.

All of the gods in Hinduism are part of the one Supreme God, Brahman. The gods and goddesses all represent parts of God, but the three most important gods are Brahma, Shiva and Vishnu.

Brahma

Brahma is called 'the creator' and everything there is came from him. He does not interfere with the normal affairs of humans or the other gods.

Today, very few people worship Brahma. He has nothing to do with life after it has been created, so he has no role in people's everyday lives.

Shiva

Shiva is called 'the destroyer', but he is not seen as bad or evil. Instead, he destroys so that re-birth can take place, just as spring cannot happen unless there is winter.

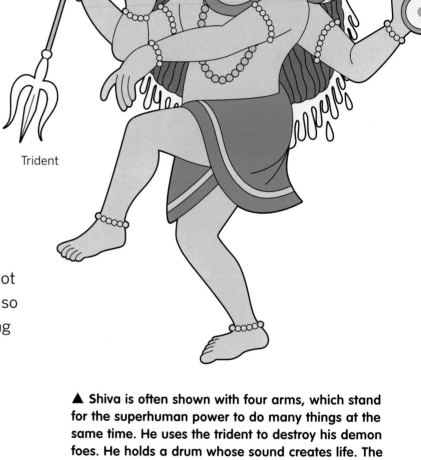

Trident

▲ Shiva is often shown with four arms, which stand for the superhuman power to do many things at the same time. He uses the trident to destroy his demon foes. He holds a drum whose sound creates life. The beads of his necklace stand for all time (past, present and future). He is often shown with a cobra, the naga which is a symbol of FERTILITY and strength, wrapped around his neck. The water flowing from his hair stands for the goddess Ganga, the River Ganges.

◄ The LINGAM is another way of showing Shiva. The word lingam means symbol. The lingam is a stone which is broad in the middle and conical towards the top. It rests on a stand called a YONI.

▶ Vishnu is recognisable by the four symbols he often carries: discus, conch, club and lotus. The discus and club are both weapons, and stand for his ability to destroy evil. The lotus stands for fertility and rebirth. The conch shell is blown in India like a trumpet during many sacred rituals. It stands for purity and goodness.

Vishnu is often shown with blue skin, which stands for the sky and the ocean. A V-shaped symbol, which stands for his footprints, appears on his forehead.

Discus

Vishnu

Vishnu is called 'the preserver'. His job is to maintain the balance between good and evil. When evil gets the upper hand, Vishnu comes down to Earth to restore the balance. This has happened nine times in the past. When he is on Earth, Vishnu takes the form of a human or an animal. These forms are called **AVATARS** of Vishnu (pages 12–13).

Because he is responsible for stability and order, Vishnu is also thought of as the god of home and family values.

◀ Brahma is the creator of the world. His four heads and four arms stand for the four points of the compass. He is often shown holding a vase of water, which stands for the water from which the universe evolved; a set of prayer beads, for counting the passage of time; a spoon which reminds us of Hindu priests and their role in making offerings; and the four Vedas, ancient sacred books of the Hindus. He is also sometimes shown with a disc and an alms bowl. He may be shown on a lotus throne, with a beard and wearing black or white clothes.

Mahadevi and the goddesses

Hindus worship hundreds of goddesses, but most are forms of Mahadevi, also called the Great Goddess, the Mother Goddess or Shakti.

The goddess Mahadevi can take a number of forms. Many of these are wives or companions to Brahma, Shiva and Vishnu. For example, Lakshmi, the wife of Vishnu, Parvati, the wife of Shiva and Saraswati, the wife of Brahma.

▶ Parvati.

▼ Lakshmi is usually shown with four arms, standing or sitting on a lotus throne, holding lotus flowers and with gold coins spilling from her hands. The lotus stands for fertility and purity, while the gold stands for wealth and prosperity.

Lakshmi

Lakshmi is Vishnu's wife. She is also the goddess of wealth, beauty and good luck. Because Lakshmi is a bringer of good luck, her image is often displayed in homes or over doorways, so that she can bring happiness and luck to everyone in the house.

Parvati

Parvati is the wife of Shiva. Her name means 'daughter of the mountain' and she is said to have been born from the rocks of the Himalaya mountains. She is the gentle and peaceful part of Mahadevi.

Parvati's obedience to her husband, Shiva, shows worshippers the kind of relationship they should have with God. She is often shown standing or sitting next to Shiva.

Saraswati

Saraswati is the wife of Brahma and the goddess of learning and the arts (see picture on page 24). It is said that she can create anything that comes into the mind of Brahma, and that she created the Sanskrit language in which the Hindu holy scriptures are written. She is also called Vagishwari, the goddess of speech.

Kali

Kali is another form of Mahadevi. But as Parvati stands for the kind and gentle side of Mahadevi, Kali stands for terror, destruction and the fear that we must overcome before we can find God. Kali is also the destroyer of evil and of demons.

Durga

Durga is another form of Mahadevi. She is also called the 'Divine Mother' because she protects people from evil and misery by destroying evil forces such as selfishness, jealousy, prejudice, hatred, anger and ego.

    She is usually shown holding weapons. These are used for the destruction of evil and the protection of good.

▲ Kali is made to look very frightening. She is usually shown wearing a tiger skin, and with tangled hair and fang-like teeth. Around her neck is a necklace of skulls. In her hands are severed heads, a dagger and a sword.

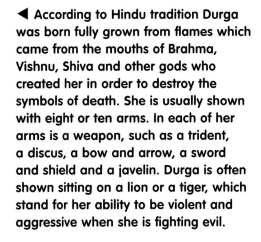

◄ According to Hindu tradition Durga was born fully grown from flames which came from the mouths of Brahma, Vishnu, Shiva and other gods who created her in order to destroy the symbols of death. She is usually shown with eight or ten arms. In each of her arms is a weapon, such as a trident, a discus, a bow and arrow, a sword and shield and a javelin. Durga is often shown sitting on a lion or a tiger, which stand for her ability to be violent and aggressive when she is fighting evil.

Avatars of Vishnu and Ganesha

There are many other important gods. These include forms of Vishnu, called avatars, and the god Ganesha.

There are hundreds of other gods and goddesses in Hinduism. For example, whenever evil gets the upper hand, Vishnu comes down to Earth to restore the balance. He has done this nine times in the past, each time in a different form, called an **AVATAR**.

◀ Krishna.

Krishna

Krishna is the eighth avatar of Vishnu, and he is worshipped by more Hindus than any other of Vishnu's forms.

Krishna represents joy, freedom and love. He is often shown as a mischievous child and many stories in the Hindu scriptures are told of his childhood.

In his adult life, Krishna was the wise hero of the ancient epic poem the **MAHABHARATA**, in which he laid down the principles of practical Hinduism.

Rama and Sita

The seventh avatar of Vishnu was Lord Rama, a princely hero who represents the qualities loyalty, bravery, strength and responsibility. He is also a role model for how to be the perfect son, husband and ruler.

▶ Hanuman, Rama and Sita.

Rama's beloved wife was Sita, a form of Lakshmi. Sita stands for the ideals of femininity, faithfulness, resilience and purity.

Rama and Sita are often shown accompanied by the monkey god Hanuman. Hanuman is the gods' messenger, and he stands for the power to achieve the impossible, the importance of duty, absolute trustworthiness and selfless service to the gods.

The Hindu epic poem, the **RAMAYANA**, tells the heroic deeds of Rama and Sita and is used as a way of teaching proper behaviour and duty (see pages 22–23).

Ganesha

Ganesha is the elephant-headed son of Shiva and Parvati, and the god of wisdom. He is also called 'the remover of obstacles' and so he is worshipped before starting any new venture, such as sitting an exam, getting married or starting a business.

One story of how Ganesha got his elephant head goes like this: One day the goddess Parvati, while bathing, created a boy out of the mud and gave him the job of guarding the entrance to her bathroom. When her husband Shiva came home, he was surprised to find a strange boy keeping him out and he cut off the boy's head in rage. Parvati broke down in utter grief and to soothe her, Shiva sent his guards to fetch the head of any sleeping being who was facing north. The guards found an elephant and brought back its head. Shiva brought Ganesha back to life and attached the elephant's head to his body. Shiva then told Ganesha that for all time, people will say his name before undertaking any venture.

▲ Ganesha's elephant head stands for gaining knowledge by listening (big ears) and thinking (large head). One of Ganesha's tusks is broken and one is whole, to show that the world is both perfect and imperfect at the same time. Ganesha's pot belly stands for the way that wisdom can help us digest whatever experiences life brings. Ganesha is often shown with one leg on the ground and the other one folded for meditation, to show a balance between the practical and spiritual life.

In his hands he holds a rope, to trap things which distract us, and a goad, to help push us along the path of wisdom. Ganesha loves sweets – his favourite is a LADOO, and he is often shown holding a sweet as a symbol of prosperity and well-being.

Murtis and shrines

Murtis are images of the gods and goddesses that are used in worship.

In mandirs, homes and other buildings, Hindus keep images of the gods and goddesses, called **MURTIS**. Hindus do not worship murtis, but use the murtis to help them feel closer to God.

Murtis

Murtis help worshippers to become closer to God in different ways. During worship, the god or goddess enters the murti and acts as a pipeline to God. This is why murtis are often treated like real people: they are dressed in lovely clothes and bathed in order to show respect to the god or goddess whose spirit has entered the murti.

The murti is also a reminder of the qualities of God. For example, a murti of Ganesha might be a reminder of the importance of wisdom. So, reciting prayers in front of a murti of Ganesha may help the worshipper to focus on wisdom and how it can be used in everyday life.

Murtis can be made of almost anything. Some are made of gold, while others are made of pottery, and still others are

▼ **Praying while standing in front of a murti of Ganesha in a mandir.**

drawings or paintings, but they all have equal value. Some images are believed to always be filled with the spirit of the god they represent. In other cases the gods have to be invited in, like a special guest. This is another reason why the murti is bathed, dressed and offered flowers and foods, in the way you would treat a special guest.

Shrines

Murtis are kept in **SHRINES**. The shrine can be thought of as the home of the god or goddess. Prayers are said, and **OFFERINGS** are left, in front of the shrine. Mandirs usually have many shrines, and most Hindu homes will have a shrine for daily worship.

At home, the shrine is the heart of the family. Inside the shrine will be the murtis of gods or goddesses which are most important to that family.

Because a shrine is a home for the gods and goddesses, the doors may be closed at night, so the gods and goddesses can 'rest'.

▼ This is a murti of the god Murugan and two of his wives. They have been dressed in lovely clothes and the shrine has been colourfully decorated. The lights and flowers are offerings for the god and goddesses.

Weblink: www.CurriculumVisions.com

Puja

Hindus show reverence through their practice of puja.

Each god or goddess is worshipped in a different way. Some instructions for conducting worship services and prayers are written down in sacred texts, and others are traditions that have grown up over time.

Worship can occur in a mandir or at home and can be conducted by a priest or by an individual person.

The word for worship is **PUJA**. Puja involves experiencing God with all of the senses. Puja may include chanting or singing songs of praise; walking around the shrine; dressing the murti and bathing it in water or milk; and making offerings of flowers, milk, incense, fire, fruit and other foods.

Performing a puja

The puja service is conducted in front of the shrine. Seeing the murti (called **DARSHAN**) and making **OFFERINGS** are the heart of puja.

The exact type of offering can be different for each god or goddess. Prayers and songs are one kind of offering. Some gods have special likes. For example, Ganesha loves to receive sweets, especially **LADOO** balls.

Whatever is offered becomes blessed by the god or goddess. After worship, the food offerings are shared by the worshippers. In this way, worshippers share the blessings of the gods and goddesses.

▲ At the beginning of the puja, a bell is rung and prayers are chanted. These sounds drive away bad thoughts and welcome the god or goddess. Prayers and hymns called 'MANTRAS of invocation' may be sung. These describe and praise God.

▲ Different offerings are made to the god or goddess. First is prayer, in the form of a chant or hymn. Then water is offered. The water is sprinkled on the feet, the hands and from head to foot of the murti. Next, offerings of sandalwood paste, raw rice mixed with kumkum (a red powder) and flowers may be made.

At home, the puja is usually led by the head of the household.

In a mandir, Hindu **PRIESTS**, called pujari, lead the puja. The difference between a puja

▲ The priest waves the light three times at the feet of the murti, then three times at the head, then three times from feet to head – in circular motions from right to left, while worshippers chant prayers. Then the lamp is waved over the worshippers as a reminder that the eternal light of God shines within each of us.

▲ After being blessed, these offerings were placed in a package for the worshipper to take away and eat. This is a way of sharing the blessing of the gods and goddesses.

▲ Other offerings may also be made, such as fruit, sweets or cooked foods.

Hindu priests

Priests are people who have studied the Hindu sacred books and learned how to conduct worship. They often go to special colleges to learn to be priests, although some people may be taught by their parents. Hindu priests can marry and have families.

In the past, only members of the highest CASTE, called Brahmans, were allowed to be priests, but this has started to change.

A large mandir may have full time priests, but the priests in smaller mandirs may have 'regular' jobs and only officiate part-time.

at home and in the mandir is that the mandir is considered to be the royal home of the gods and so everything is much more lavish.

Puja is usually followed by a ceremony called **AARTI**. We will learn about this on the following pages.

Aarti

Aarti is a form of prayer, usually performed three times a day.

In the mandir, aarti is usually performed three or four times a day: at sunrise, during the morning, at lunchtime and at sundown. At home, aarti may be performed each time there is worship. During aarti, light from wicks soaked in **GHEE** (clarified butter) is offered to the gods and goddesses.

The essence of the aarti ceremony is that all day long God offers us light – the light of the sun, the light of life, the light of blessings. Aarti is a time to say "thank you," by offering light and devotion to the gods and goddesses.

The pujari lights a three or five-wick lamp and waves it in front of the murti. He then offers the lamp to each worshipper in turn. Worshippers place their hands over the flames, then pass their hands in front of their face and over their head. In this way, they are sharing the blessing of light with the gods.

▼ In this photo a priest is offering the aarti lamp to worshippers in a mandir. Sometimes, a worshipper passes around the aarti lamp instead. You can see that the boy in the middle is placing his hands near the flame. The priest on the left is saying a prayer before he shares the flame.

▲ A worshipper is passing around the aarti flames. Here, the wicks are set on a tray instead of in a lamp. The coins on the tray are offerings that will be used to buy things like milk and ghee for giving to the gods and goddesses.

Sacred texts

Hindus do not have one 'Holy Book' like many other religions, but many texts.

There are two main groups of Hindu sacred teachings. The first are called **SRUTI**, which means 'things that are heard'. Sruti are teachings that are believed to have come directly from God. The sruti teachings are also called the **VEDIC SCRIPTURE**. The expression 'Vedic' is a Sanskrit word which means knowledge or revelation.

The second group of sacred texts are called **SMRITI**, which means 'things that are remembered'. They were composed long ago by scholars and poets.

Vedic scriptures

These are the most important Hindu sacred texts. They are thousands of years old and contain hymns, incantations, and rituals from ancient India.

▶ This painting is from a sixteenth century PERSIAN translation of the Hindu epic story, the Mahabharata. It shows a part of the Mahabharata where the hero Arjuna is challenged to a battle by Suratha. Arjuna's charioteer is Lord Krishna.

There are four books of Vedic scripture: the Rig Veda, Sama Veda, Yajur Veda and Atharva Veda.

Rig means ritual, and the Rig Veda contains mainly hymns and prayers used in the worship of the gods. Yajur means ceremony, and the Yajur Veda mainly describes how to perform worship rituals. Sama means singing; the Sama Veda contains religious chants, as well as strict rules on how to chant them properly.

Atharva means 'a priest who knows the secret lore'; the Atharva Vedas describe many different kinds of worship practices to use when worshipping the gods and goddesses. The Atharva Vedas also contain information about Hindu methods of medicine and other practical things.

All of the Vedic teachings are supposed to encourage people to understand that God is all around us. Through following the chants and the way of life described in the Vedas, individuals can make a personal connection with God.

The Upanishads

The **UPANISHADS** are ancient books that discuss and add to the knowledge in the Vedas. The word Upanishad is Sanskrit and means 'to sit down near', and they are based on the teachings of gurus whose students sat close by them and listened to their words.

The Upanishads are meant to inspire people to learn from the Vedas. The Upanishads explain how the soul can be united with God through contemplation and meditation, as well as through the law of karma.

The Brahmanas

These texts give instructions for the proper way to worship the gods, including how to perform rituals and prayers.

The Aranyakas

These books discuss philosophy. These are called the 'forest books' because in ancient times these topics were discussed secretly in the forest.

Smriti Texts

The smriti texts are more popular and easy to understand than the sruti texts. They include books of laws, **PURANAS** (myths, stories and legends) and epic stories.

The epic poems and stories contain moral and spiritual ideas and lessons. The two most important are the **MAHABHARATA** and the **RAMAYANA**.

The Puranas

These texts include stories of the gods and goddesses, tales of the creation, destruction and recreation of the world and information on subjects such as science and astronomy.

The Mahabharata

The Mahabharata contains 100,000 verses in 18 chapters. It tells the story of Lord Krishna, the eighth avatar of Vishnu. The main story of the Mahabharata tells the story of a rivalry between groups of cousins – the Kauravas and the Pandavas. At the end is a great battle that is won by the heroes – the Pandavas. This stands for the victory of good over evil. Woven within the Mahabharata are dozens of other stories and hundreds of characters.

The Mahabharata stresses the horror of war and the teachings of the Hindu dharma. One section of the Mahabharata, called the **BHAGVAD GITA**, is one of the most popular stories in Hinduism.

Bhagvad Gita

The words Bhagvad Gita mean 'song of God'. This section of the Mahabharata contains a discussion between Lord Krishna and the hero Arjuna about human nature and the purpose of life.

The Bhagvad Gita begins as Arjuna and Krishna are riding out to battle. As Arjuna looks at the opposing armies and sees his relatives, teachers and friends fighting on either side, he is heartsick at the thought of killing these beloved persons. He turns to Krishna for advice. Through their discussion, Krishna describes how to achieve moksha through duty and devotion to God.

Ramayana

The Ramayana, which means 'the Romance of Rama', is made up of 96,000 verses in seven chapters. It tells the life story of prince Rama of Ayodhya, the seventh avatar of the god Vishnu, whose wife Sita

▼ This picture shows a scene from the Ramayana – the coronation of King Rama. On the left, Rama is consecrated King. The right hand side shows Rama and Sita giving out gold and jewels to those who helped them.

is abducted by the demon Ravana. Woven into the story are teachings of ancient Hindu wise men and gurus.

Rama is the heir to the kingdom of Ayodhya. But his stepmother conspires to stop him getting to the throne and instead he is exiled to the forest. His wife, Sita, and his brother, Lakshmana, follow him.

While in the forest, Sita is carried off by Ravana, the demon king of Lanka. In their search for Sita, the brothers battle evil with the help of the monkey general, Hanuman, and his monkey army. Eventually, Ravana

is slain by Rama and Sita is rescued, the couple are reunited and Rama rules in peace.

In the Ramayana are teachings on the proper way for kings to behave to their subjects; on how husbands and wives should treat each other; and on how to be faithful to our families and those we love. The story emphasises that proper behaviour by everyone in society will lead to peace and harmony for all.

The holiday of **DIWALI** celebrates Rama's triumphant return to his kingdom (see picture on page 22).

▼ This picture shows a scene from the Ramayana called 'the giving of the ring'. Seated on a rocky outcrop are Rama and Lakshmana, with the monkey army below them and springing away to the sides. Rama gives Hanuman his ring as a token by which Sita can recognise him.

A Hindu way of life

Hindu worship is about more than gods and stories, it is also a guide for living in harmony with the world around us.

Because God is everywhere, worship is a part of everyday life/ Instead of going to a mandir at a set time each week or each day, Hindus worship whenever they feel the need to. Because the Hindu gods and goddesses are everywhere, honouring them is woven into everyday life in many ways.

For example, a school student may worship the goddess Saraswati, goddess of wisdom and the arts. Worshipping the goddess before an exam helps the student to focus on wisdom and their own ability. After the exam, the student also thanks the goddess through worship.

At other times, people may worship in order to ask a god or goddess to help them. For example, if a husband and wife want a child, they might worship Chandra, the Moon god, who brings fertility.

▼ A priest dresses the murti of a goddess in preparation for worship in a mandir.

◀ The goddess Saraswati.

Hindu values

Hinduism is more than a way of worship, it is also a way of everyday living. For example, Hinduism teaches the principle of **NON-VIOLENCE**, which prohibits harming any animal. This is why many Hindus are **VEGETARIAN**.

Many Hindus also believe that the cow is a living symbol of Mother Earth. Cows are also seen as symbols of Krishna, the eighth avatar of Vishnu,

▶ Many people worship at home in front of personal or family shrines.

▼ For many Hindus, cows are sacred and must not be killed.

who spent part of his happy childhood as a cowherd. So, to feed a cow or care for a cow is a way of worshipping Krishna.

In ancient times, and for rural families today, cows are very important. They provide a lot for families, including milk, milk products, labour and dung (used as fuel). Because a cow gives all its possessions for the benefit of others, they were thought of as one of the most important parts of the family. These are some of the reasons why Hindu holy scriptures prohibit the killing of cows.

Hinduism also teaches that duty and proper behaviour are important in helping us to reach moksha. So, showing respect to your family and treating others with kindness is another part of being Hindu that is practised everyday and all the time.

Personal gods and goddesses

Many families have household shrines. Although children grow up following family beliefs, they are encouraged as young adults to make their own choices of which gods or goddesses they find personally inspiring. So, the household shrine may contain many murtis, or there may be several small individual shrines in one household.

Personal symbols

Many Hindus wear or use individual symbols of their faith.

There are hundreds of different symbols used in Hinduism. Some of these are found on murtis, such as the things the gods and goddesses are holding. Other symbols are used by people in their everyday lives to demonstrate their faith. Here are some of these types of symbols.

▲ This boy is putting a tilaka of sandalwood on his brother's forehead after worship.

Aum

Hindus believe that God first created the sound "**AUM**", and that the vibrations of the sound caused the world to be created. So, Hindus often chant this sound during worship and meditation. You can see the word aum (above right) written on many mandirs and Hindu artworks.

Tilaka

The **TILAKA** is a sign of being Hindu. It is made of ash or coloured and scented paste that has been blessed by the gods and goddesses. Worshippers may put tilaka on as a reminder that God is always with them, or as a sign that they are Hindu.

The tilaka is put on the forehead, in-between the eyes, in a spot believed to be important for wisdom and concentration. Many people believe that this spot controls all of our thoughts and actions. The tilaka is a paste, often made of sandalwood, which is cooling, so that it will help keep the mind cool and calm.

Bindi

Women sometimes wear a type of tilaka called a **BINDI**. The bindi may stand for different things, such as whether or not the woman is married, or it may be just a decoration. The bindi is also a reminder of a person's Hindu faith.

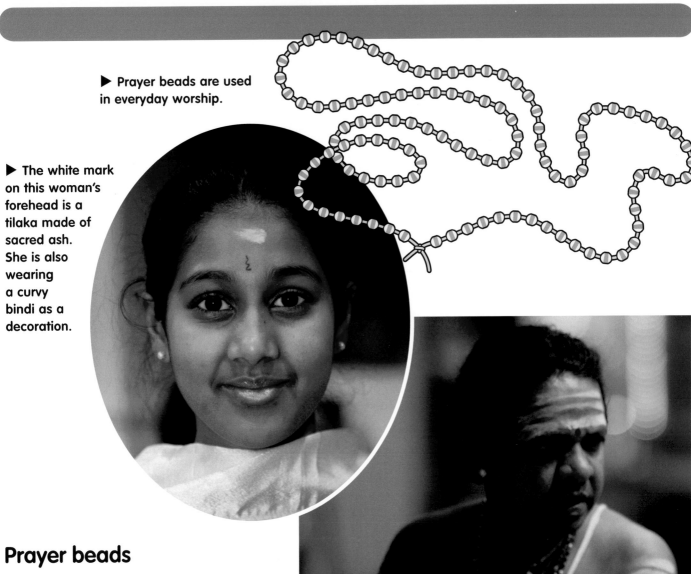

▶ Prayer beads are used in everyday worship.

▶ The white mark on this woman's forehead is a tilaka made of sacred ash. She is also wearing a curvy bindi as a decoration.

Prayer beads

Hindu prayer beads are called **MALA**, which means 'garland of flowers'. The beads are made from a dried fruit called rudraksha, which means 'Shiva's Eye'. It is said that Shiva sat in open-eyed meditation for 1,000 years. When he finally blinked, the tears that streamed from his eyes became rudraksha seeds.

There are usually 109 beads on a strand. These stand for the 108 names of Shiva, plus an extra bead. The beads are most often used to count prayers to Shiva, Ganesha and Krishna, and to recite the names of Shiva. The surface of the seed is rough and represents the austere life the Shiva worshipper should follow.

▲ There are many different shapes for tilaka. For example, people who worship Shiva apply three horizontal lines of sacred ash on their forehead. This is to remind themselves that God is three important things: creator, preserver and destroyer.

People who worship Vishnu apply three vertical lines of sandalwood, or a red spot surrounded by two lines, which stand for Vishnu's feet. This is a sign that Vishnu is standing with the worshipper, looking after them.

Hindu celebrations

Hindu communities celebrate many different festivals and holidays.

▲▶ These photos show a Sri Lankan New Year festival in a Hindu community in England. Different communities of Hindus celebrate different festivals.

Festivals and celebrations are a very important part of Hinduism. There are festivals dedicated to many of the gods and goddesses. In addition to these, there are festivals which celebrate traditional events like the harvest, the coming of spring and the New Year. Each festival is a joyous celebration of life. Most are celebrated with worship in the mandir, parades, open-air festivals, special foods and music.

◀ During the Maha Sivarathri festival, special offerings are made in a fire in the mandir.

Seasonal festivals

Some Hindu festivals celebrate the change of the seasons. For example, the festival of **HOLI** (in February or March) welcomes the spring and celebrates the Hindu New Year. It is also a celebration in honour of Krishna. People light bonfires and throw coloured powder and water at each other.

Mid-January, considered to be a lucky time of year, is celebrated with the festival of good fortune, Makar Sankranti, when children fly colourful kites.

Festivals for gods and goddesses

Throughout the Hindu year, many festivals are held to celebrate the birthday, marriage or important events in the lives of the gods and goddesses. Some of these festivals are local, while others are celebrated around India and elsewhere.

One of the most important festivals is Diwali, the festival of light (also called deepavali). This festival occurs on the night of the Full Moon in October or November.

It celebrates a story told in the Ramayana of the return of Rama from exile and of the way the light of knowledge conquers the darkness of ignorance. Homes and streets are decorated with oil lamps, candles and coloured lights.

The festival of Maha Sivarathri is dedicated to the god Shiva and is celebrated during the night and day that come just before the New Moon in February.

Ganesha's birthday is celebrated each year at the festival of Ganesh Chaturthi in August or September. Statues of the god are paraded through the streets and then thrown in to a lake or stream, taking with them any misfortune or bad thoughts.

The festival of nine nights (Navaratri, or Durga puja) takes place in September or October in honour of the goddess Durga. The festival celebrates a story of how Durga defeated a demon. Many people fast during part of this festival. The day after the festival is another festival, Dussehra, which celebrates Rama's victory over Ravana in the Ramayana.

Glossary

AARTI The ritual performed at the end of worship. Aarti is a Sanskrit word which means 'to end'. It is a way of finishing the worship ceremony, of thanking God, and of asking forgiveness for any mistakes.

ARTHA The idea that we should strive to be successful in everything we do. This will free us to have more time to concentrate on God. Artha is not just money, but also other kinds of wealth that cannot be measured, such as love and family.

AUM The sacred sound that was said by Brahma in order to create the universe.

AVATAR The human (or sometimes animal) form of a god or goddess. When the gods come to Earth they take the form of an avatar.

BHAGVAD GITA Part of the Mahabharata, or Hindu scripture that tells how to achieve moksha.

BINDI A mark on the forehead used by women to show their marital status or just for decoration.

BRAHMAN God as the Supreme Creator of the universe, the ultimate reality, which has no shape and cannot be known by ordinary people.

CASTE The way that traditional Hindu society was organised. Each person was born into a certain social group.

DARSHAN Viewing and being in the presence of the god or goddess during worship.

DHARMA The correct path. This is a code of conduct for living your life and worshipping according to God's will.

DIWALI Meaning 'festival of lights' this popular holiday celebrates the part of the Ramayana when Rama returns from exile.

ENLIGHTENMENT Another way of saying achieving moksha, or being free from the cycle of death and rebirth.

FERTILITY Having offspring. When we say something is very fertile, that means it has a lot of offspring.

GHEE Clarified butter, made by removing the milk solids (whey) from butter to leave pure milk fat.

GODS AND GODDESSES Different forms or parts of God. Each god and goddess represents different parts of God.

GURU A wise or holy person. The word guru means 'one who lights the darkness' and gurus are spiritual teachers who teach others how to reach moksha.

HINDU A person who believes in and follows Hinduism.

HINDUISM A religion which teaches that the ultimate goal is to free oneself from the cycle of death and rebirth and unite with God. Hinduism teaches that there are many different ways to do this.

HOLI A festival that celebrates the spring. It celebrates Krishna's defeat of the winter demon, Holika.

KARMA The idea that what we do in this life has an effect on our future lives. It can be thought of as fate. A person can create bad karma or good karma through doing bad or good in this life.

LADOO A type of sweet usually made from ghee (clarified butter), sugar, chickpea flour and flavourings. It is said to be Ganesha's favourite sweet.

LAW OF KARMA The idea that every soul is reborn over and over until it has learned how to stop creating any karma. Then it will join with God.

LINGAM A form of the god Shiva which stands for male creative energy.

MAHABHARATA A Hindu epic poem and religious scripture which tells the story of rivalry between two families. In the story are woven lessons on duty, devotion and the meaning of life.

MALA Prayer beads used during meditation.

MANDIR A Hindu place of worship. Also called a temple.

MANTRA A phrase which is repeated over and over in order to help focus the mind. It may contain sacred words or the names of God. Repeating a mantra can help lead to moksha, or enlightenment.

MEDITATION A way of sitting quietly and emptying the mind of everyday thoughts in order to concentrate only on God or on achieving moksha or enlightenment.

MOKSHA Being free from the cycles of death and rebirth; the goal of Hinduism. Also called enlightenment. When a soul reaches moksha, it joins with God.

MURTI An image (statue, picture, and so on) of a god or goddess.

NON-VIOLENCE The idea that any kind of violence (including killing animals for food) creates bad karma so we should never use violence for any reason.

OFFERING Giving a gift to a god or goddess to be blessed. The gods and goddesses do not need or demand gifts, instead, they are a way of sharing blessings with the gods and goddesses.

PERSIAN An ancient kingdom founded in modern day Iran. The Persian, or Moghul, kingdom ruled modern day India and Pakistan in the 16th and 17th centuries.

PRIEST In Hinduism, a person who has been trained to perform worship rituals.

PUJA Hindu worship rituals to show devotion to gods and goddesses.

PURANA One of the most important smriti books of sacred Hindu writings.

RAMAYANA A great Hindu epic poem that tells the story of Prince Rama, an avatar of Vishnu. Woven into the story are lessons on love, war and peace and how good overcomes evil.

REINCARNATION The idea that our souls are reborn over and over again in new bodies. In Hinduism, each soul is reincarnated over and over until it learns to stop creating karma and joins with God.

RIG VEDA The oldest and one of the most important of the four Hindu religious scriptures called the Vedas. It contains hymns used in worship.

SANSKRIT The language used for writing in ancient India. Many ancient Hindu texts are written in Sanskrit.

SHRINE A home for a god or goddess. Murtis are placed in shrines, which may be big or small, simple or highly decorated.

SMRITI 'Things remembered'; these are ancient sacred writings on topics such as ritual, law and stories of the gods and goddesses.

SOUL The part of us that lives on in each rebirth. The part of each person that makes them unique.

SRUTI 'Things heard'; these are sacred writings that are believed to be things ancient wise men heard from God.

TILAKA A sacred mark placed on the forehead after worship as a reminder of the god's or goddess' presence.

TRIMURTI The trio of the most important Hindu gods: Brahma, Shiva and Vishnu.

UPANISHAD Sacred books based on the teachings of ancient gurus or wise men. They explain moksha and reincarnation.

VEDIC SCRIPTURE Hindu religious scriptures, including sruti and smriti books. Veda is a Sanskrit word which means knowledge, truth or wisdom.

VEGETARIAN A person who does not eat meat. Some vegetarians also do not eat fish or any animal products, such as milk and eggs.

YOGA A religious practice as well as a type of exercise. It involves breathing exercises, and placing the body in different positions that help to make the body healthier and also help to improve concentration. If used only as an exercise it can improve health. If used as a religious practice it can help achieve moksha.

YONI A stand for the lingam. It stands for female creative energy.

Index

aarti 17, 18–19, 30
artha 6, 7, 30
aum 26, 30
avatar 9, 12–13, 21, 22, 25, 30

Bhagvad Gita 22, 30
bindi 26, 27, 30
Brahma 8, 9, 10, 11
Brahman 4, 8, 30
Brahmanas 21
Brahmans 17

caste 17, 30

darshan 16, 30
dharma 6, 7, 22, 30
Diwali 23, 29, 30
Durga 11, 29

enlightenment 6, 7, 30

fertility 8, 9, 10, 24, 30

Ganesha 12, 13, 14, 16, 27, 29
ghee 18, 19, 30
gods and goddesses 4, 30
    and throughout
guru 4, 21, 23, 30

Hanuman 12, 13, 23
Hindu 4, 30 and throughout

Hinduism 4, 30 and throughout
Holi 29, 30

Kali 11
karma 2, 6–7, 21, 30
Krishna 12, 20, 21, 22, 25, 27, 29

ladoo 13, 16, 30
Lakshmi 10, 13
law of karma 6, 21, 30
lingam 8, 30

Mahabharata 12, 20, 21–22, 30
Mahadevi 10–11
Maha Sivarathri 29
mala 27, 30
mandir 2, 5, 14, 16, 17, 18, 24, 26, 28,
    29, 30
mantra 16, 30
meditation 2, 4, 13, 21, 26, 27, 31
moksha 2, 6, 7, 22, 25, 31
murti 14–15, 16, 17, 18, 24, 25, 26, 31
Murugan 15

non-violence 6, 24, 31

offering 5, 9, 14, 15, 16, 17, 18, 19,
    29, 31
Parvati 10, 11, 13
Persian 20, 31
priest 5, 9, 16–17, 18, 21, 24, 31

puja 6, 16–17, 29, 31
pujari 17, 18
Puranas 21, 31

Rama 12–13, 22–23, 29
Ramayana 13, 22–23, 29, 31
reincarnation 2, 4, 7, 31
Rig Veda 4, 20, 31

Sanskrit 6, 10, 20, 21, 31
Saraswati 10–11, 24
Shiva 8, 10, 11, 13, 27, 29
shrine 14–15, 16, 25, 31
Sita 12–13, 22–23
smriti 20, 21, 31
soul 2, 4, 6, 21, 31
sruti 20, 21, 31

tilaka 26, 27, 31
trimurti 8–9, 31

Upanishad 21, 31

Vedic scripture 20–21, 31
vegetarian 24, 31
Vishnu 8, 9, 10, 11, 12–13, 21, 22,
    25, 27

yoni 8, 31
yoga 4, 31

Curriculum Visions

Curriculum Visions is a registered trademark of Atlantic Europe Publishing Company Ltd.

There's more online
See our great collection of page-turning books and multimedia resources at:

www.CurriculumVisions.com

(CurriculumVisions.com is a subscription web site)

A CVP Book
This second edition © Atlantic Europe Publishing 2011

First reprint 2014. First edition 2005.

Authors
Brian Knapp, BSc, PhD, and Lisa Magloff, MA

Religious Adviser
Dr Sarbani Mukherjee and Dr AK Ghosh

Senior Designer
Adele Humphries, BA

Acknowledgements
The publishers would like to thank Dr Sarbani Mukherjee and Dr AK Ghosh for their help and advice.

Photographs
The Earthscape Picture Library, except pages 20, 22 and 23 British Library, and page 25 Chantal Boulanger.

Illustrations
David Woodroffe

Designed and produced by
Atlantic Europe Publishing Ltd

Printed in China by
WKT Company Ltd

Hindu faith and practice 2nd edition – Curriculum Visions
A CIP record for this book is available from the British Library

ISBN 978 1 86214 687 7

This product is manufactured from sustainable managed forests. For every tree cut down at least one more is planted.